KT-366-409

THE TRANSFORMING EXPERIENCE

BY

H. G. TUNNICLIFF, B.A.

Author of *The Personality of Paul, A Child's Pilgrim's Progress*, &c.

LONDON

THE EPWORTH PRESS

J. ALFRED SHARP.

First Edition - 1931

Made and Printed in
Great Britain by the Devonshire Press, Torquay.

To
JOHN CHEESBROUGH TURTON

PREFACE

THESE chapters are simple, and only touch the fringes of ' a deep where all our thoughts are drowned.' Their aim is to catch the spirit and outlook of men and women in different ages and places who have entered into a transforming experience of God in Christ Jesus ; who have found a Saviour and Friend in Jesus, to whom God has become splendidly real and intimately nigh, and in and through whom His Spirit has mightily wrought.

I owe an immeasurable debt to Paper No. 4 of the Fellowship of the Kingdom Series, and to the men with whom in the rich fellowship of thought and prayer I have sought to explore its heights and depths. Anything of value in these pages has sprung from that source.

Daily readings are appended to each chapter, the seventh day being reserved for re-reading of the main theme. For such as will use the book for Group work, I would suggest that the seventh day would most appropriately be that on which the Group meets. Each chapter should be read carefully and assimilated by every member before the meeting.

Be it ever remembered that this is no academic affair, remote from daily life. The Quest for the transforming experience of the Living Jesus if honestly, patiently, and steadily pursued is bound to end in creating Crusaders, for the experience is so amazing that it cannot be bottled up. It evokes the warm and enthusiastic *cri de coeur*,

O let me commend my Saviour to you,

When the tides of the Spirit are flowing, there is no dearth of Christian workers or lack of Christian witness.

H. G. T.

PAIGNTON,
February, 1931.

CONTENTS

THE NEW LIFE

THE
TRANSFORMING EXPERIENCE

I

THE NEW LIFE

In his *New Studies in Mystical Religion*, Dr. Rufus Jones has truly written, ' What we find when we go back to the birth of our religion is that it began as a new way of life. It was in the first instance an experience of God. It was saturated with the consciousness of God.' That experience was the rich possession of the early Church, and it has always been the foundation of every real revival of religion. The first believers never lost the glow that strangely warmed their hearts on the transforming day of Pentecost. They had awakened then to a new and thrilling realization of a living and ever present Jesus, of an energising Holy Spirit, and of a God nigh at hand, no pale metaphysical abstraction, no distant deity, but working for, and with, and through them. That glow cheered and fortified them in days of gloom, hardship, and disappointment. Outside lay the pagan world, overwhelming in its numbers, titanic in its power, cruel, implacable, and licentious, but within there was Jesus. They found solid comfort and abiding strength in constantly reminding one another of the vitalizing truth, ' Jesus Christ is the same, yesterday, to-day, and for ever.'

They had entered into a new way of life ; they had

experienced re-birth, and theirs was the thrill and the ardour of youth. Old habits were transformed, old beliefs were revised, old truths were re-stated. Life was thrilling because wondrous powers had been liberated and wondrous joys experienced. The apostles spoke of their teaching as words of life. Peter at Pentecost designated Jesus as ' Prince ' or ' Author ' of life, and that triumphant note reverberates throughout the apostolic writings. Dr. Cairns has thus recalled the glow of that experience : ' Mommsen has summed up the condition of the Graeco-Roman world in a memorable sentence. The world, he says, on the closing page of his History, was growing old, and not even Caesar could make it young again. . . . What Caesar was unable to do, Christ has done. The Christian Church has lived spiritually on the New Testament ever since, because of its vitalizing power. Yet the New Testament is only the fragment of an age written by " a new race," as they loved to call themselves, spiritually more alive than ours. The trumpets of the spring are sounding through all its pages.'

The paths by which men and women entered into this new life were many and varied. There were mass movements in Jerusalem and Samaria ; the Ethiopian Eunuch found Jesus in the lonely desert ; Saul of Tarsus met with his Saviour on the Damascus Road ; Cornelius, with his family and his friends, was baptized in his own house ; Lydia's conversion was gradual, like the breaking of a pearly dawn after the blackness of night—whose heart the Lord opened —whilst her fellow townsman, the jailer, found God under the stress of a terrific experience. But they

all found God, or rather, as Paul says in one of his
significant emendations, were found of Him.

The members of the early Church had entered into
a new and tender relationship with God. They
realized that Jesus had come to reveal to man the
true nature of God, and that revelation brought new
hope and confidence. He was the Seeker and the
Lover who never lets us go. 'He that hath seen
Me hath seen the Father,' was one of the tender
farewell messages of Jesus, and that meant reassur-
ance. They had a new insight into the loving heart
of their Father as they recalled to one another the
amazing earthly life of Jesus, so full of welcome for
the sinful and outcast, of tenderness for the sick and
sorrowful, of interest in little children, of love, not
for Jew only, but for all mankind. They had made
the glorious discovery that they were children of
God the Father, not subjects of a capricious despot
or slaves of a cruel taskmaster. The divine life had
been communicated to them, and they were transformed—born from above.

This new life was 'In Christ,' or 'in Christ Jesus.'
Some such expression is used no less than eighty
times in the New Testament. As Dr. Glover has
written : ' Before the Gospels were written, men
spoke of the Spirit of Jesus as an active force amongst
them. We may criticize their phrase and their
psychology as we like, but they were speaking of
something they knew, something they had seen and
felt, and it is that " something " which changed the
course of history. . . . Of His immediate followers
we know almost nothing, but it was they who passed
Him on to the next generation, consciously in their

preaching, and unconsciously in their lives which He had transformed, which had gained from Him something of the power of His own life. The Church was a nexus of quickened and redeemed personalities, men and women in whom Christ lived. So Paul wrote of it. A century later another nameless Christian spoke of Christ being born every day over and over again in the hearts of believers, and it would be hard to correct the statement.'

The men and women of the early Church knew the joy of the constant companionship of a living Friend. Many of them had passed through the dreadful darkness of those terrible and bitter hours that succeeded the tragedy of Calvary. At that time of gloom and disappointment it seemed as if Ichabod were written large upon the moral universe, and as if God had deserted His own. The dejection of the two who walked the Emmaus road was typical, ' The chief priests and our rulers delivered Him up to be condemned to death, and crucified Him. But we hoped that it was He which should redeem Israel.' No wonder that ' they stood still, looking sad.' Their hopes were shattered and all progress seemed to be arrested by the dragging chains of leaden sorrow.

But to their night of weeping had been added the morn of joy. They had experienced the glory and the gleam of the Resurrection bringing renewed contact and communion with their Lord. Then on the day of Pentecost there had come the thrilling and transfiguring awareness of the Spiritual Presence of Jesus—the Real Presence. The promise of the Upper Room, made on the eve of Calvary, had been wondrously verified in the very place in which it had been uttered, ' I will not leave you orphans : I come unto you. Yet a little while and the world beholdeth me no more ; but ye behold me : because I live, ye shall live also. In that day ye shall know that I am in my Father, and ye in me, and I in you.'

The Spirit of Jesus was henceforth to be their constant Guide and Companion. Their loneliness was to be for ever banished, and their ignorance was to be dispelled by the Spirit of Truth and Discernment, available for every crisis. They still were hampered by their Jewish prejudices and preconceptions, but, as Paul's changed mind about the imminent return of Jesus shows, they grew not only in love and grace, but also in knowledge. Jesus was with them as the shining centre of their fellowship. Too often we limit the promise, ' Where two or three are gathered together in my name, there am I in the midst of them,' to merely ecclesiastical assemblies, but the early Church fell into no such pit of error. They found Jesus present in the little group of friends, in the family, in the daily toil and the evening leisure. The saying of Jesus, recovered for us at Oxyrhyncus, must have been familiar to the slaves and working men of the early Church : ' Jesus saith, wherever there are two, they are not without God ; and wherever there is one alone, I say, I am with him. Raise the stone and there shalt thou find Me ; cleave the wood and there am I.'

In emphasizing the place of the Cross in the thought and preaching of the apostolic age, there is considerable danger of overlooking the suggestive fact that not only did the apostles and believers remember the dying Jesus, they also preached the living Jesus. Paul's correction is significant, ' It is Christ who died, nay rather, who was raised from the dead ' (Rom. viii. 34).

The incredible experiences that had followed the first Easter could never be forgotten, and to those who had been present in the upper room on the day of Pentecost there had come the perfect and full assurance of the ever present Jesus. Theirs was the discovery made centuries later by Thomas à Kempis: ' To be without Jesus is a grievous hell ; and to be with Jesus, a sweet paradise. If Jesus be with thee, no enemy shall be able to hurt thee. He that findeth Jesus, findeth a good treasure, yea, a Good above all good. . . . Most poor is he who liveth without Jesus ; and he is most rich who is well with Jesus.'

This rich experience has been the elevating and energizing possession of true Christians in all ages. With Rothe and John Wesley they could joyfully declare

> Now I have found the ground wherein
> Sure my soul's anchor may remain.

Of James Denholm Brash his son has written : ' No miser could have hugged to himself his gold more eagerly then he daily clung to the treasures and joys of his communion with the Lord. His life was so spontaneous, so hilarious, so conventionless—and yet so splendidly disciplined. The locked study-door, the Bible with the well-worn binding, thumbed and tear-stained, the re-bound and carefully marked hymn-book, all told that tale. No one more eagerly devoured the morning paper, but he had always first talked with the Master and mused over his Bible. He kept his morning tryst with the Lord, and throughout the day did not lose the sense of His presence. It was this which gave him that breeziness which made one think of moors and hills and wind-swept places.'

The sense of the presence of God has always made all things new for those to whom it has come with the gladness of a sweet surprise. Saul Kane's experience, of which Mr. John Masefield has sung in ' The Everlasting Mercy ' is no mere poetic phantasy, but a sober fact of history.

Etienne de Grellet, the young French nobleman knew it, and has thus borne his testimony : ' My brother and myself were invited to dine in the company of these Friends, at Colonel Corsa's. There was a religious opportunity after dinner, in which several communications were made. I could hardly understand a word of what was said, but, as Deborah Darby began to address my brother and myself, it seemed as if the Lord opened my outward ear, and my heart. She seemed like one reading the pages of my heart, with clearness describing how it had been, and how it was with me. O what sweetness did I then feel ! It was indeed a memorable day. I was like one introduced into a new world ; the creation, and all things around me, bore a different aspect, my heart glowed with love to all.'

The young nobleman was finding the truth of William Penn's declaration, ' Receive His leaven, and it will change thee ; His medicine and it will cure thee. . . . Yield up the body, soul and spirit to Him that maketh all things new : new heavens and new earth, new love, new joy, new peace, new works, a new life and conversation.'

Moody bears the same witness. ' I remember the morning on which I came out of my room after I had first trusted Christ. I thought the old sun shone a good deal brighter than it ever had before. I thought that it was just smiling upon me ; and as I walked out upon Boston Common and heard the birds singing in the trees, I thought they were all singing a song to me. Do you know, I fell in love with the birds. I had never cared for them before. It seemed to me I was in love with all creation.'

Or let a modern girl speak (her witness has been passed on by Miriam Gray, the nom-de-plume of a heroic Christian woman well known to the present writer) : ' Walking or cycling, the one thought that is constantly passing through my mind is, " He is here." I have looked at the daisies on the lawn and seen—God ; I have heard the cuckoo singing in the wood, and nearly burst with happiness as I have heard—God ; and as I was walking home after class to-day (with a new skirt all draggled with wet, and new brown shoes gone black in the rain !) I looked up at the sky and, without meaning to, I said, " BLESS HIM ! " To realize God is there, and to have Him for your Friend—well, this is LIFE.'

Dr. R. W. Dale and Canon Raven bear their witness to the difference made by a consciousness of the living Jesus, and the latest witness of all is a Cambridge girl who writes over the pseudonym of ' Elizabeth ' : ' At the next Group meeting I was conscious of the presence of God as never before : gradually it focused in the centre of the Group, and

I saw Christ standing there, sharing in the Group.
It was no trick of tired nerves ; of that I am sure.
I had prayed for an assurance of the reality of God,
and I received it in a way I had never dreamt of.
And next day I woke with a feeling of peace and joy—
and a knowledge and assurance that God is real and
true for me.'

There is much glib talk of revival, but true revival
will only come when men and women who profess
to be Christians have entered into the transforming
experience of God in Christ Jesus. The ages, differing
in language, in philosophic thought, in environment,
all unite in triumphant witness to this.

> Warm, sweet, tender, even yet
> A present help is He ;
> And faith hath still its Olivet,
> And love its Galilee.

The Cambridge Group asks, ' How can we sum-
marize our experience ? ' and then supplies this
answer :

' We had had to sacrifice nothing of our modernity
of outlook. We had never been consciously disloyal
to our scientific training and ideals. We had not
" preferred edification to truth." We had not dismissed our problems, psychological or otherwise.
We had simply sought the God who is in Jesus Christ
by ways neither old-fashioned nor new-fangled, but
eternal. We had found that " HE IS, AND THAT
HE IS A REWARDER OF THEM THAT SEEK AFTER
HIM." Let the capital letters suggest the first-class
importance of this glad discovery for us.'

DAILY READINGS

1. Luke xxiv. 5, 6 ; Acts ii. 24 ; Hebrews x. 19-23.
2. Acts iv. 33 ; xvii. 18, 31 ; Romans i. 4.
3. 2 Cor. v. 11-21.
4. John xiv. 18 ; Matthew xxviii. 20 ; Galatians i. 11, 12.
5. 1 John i. 1-4.
6. 1 John v. 11-21.

QUESTIONARY

1. How did John Wesley enter into this new and transforming experience ? Is that the way for our generation ?
2. Is this experience limited only to people of mystical temperament, or is it available for all ?
3. What do we really mean by ' Pentecostal Power ' ?

THE JOY OF THE TRANSFORMING EXPERIENCE

II

THE JOY OF THE TRANSFORMING EXPERIENCE

DONN BYRNE, in his *Brother Saul*, has pictured with truth and charm the men and women of the early Church : ' Paul's catechumens were great-limbed and free. It was as though he had given them the freedom of the starry roads. They girt their loins and looked out on the world as mariners look over the waters, keen-eyed and confident. And they were merry from goodness of heart.'

There lies the tragedy of one of the causes of the estrangement of the ' outsider ' from the Christian Church. He woefully misunderstands the true situation, regarding the Christian as a ' kill-joy.' A merry Christmas seems perfectly natural to him, but a merry Christian is not to be thought of. But the ' outsider ' of the early days was compelled to recognize the Christian by his very exuberance and hilarity. Men and women who had passed from death unto life, from fetters to freedom, from sin to salvation, were filled with boundless rapture and transcendent ecstasy. Religion was so real, God was so gloriously near, that they could not but be buoyant. Browning's lines well express their glad experience :

> I know Thee, who hast kept my path, and made
> Light for me in the darkness, tempering sorrow
> So that it reached me like a solemn joy.

So much emphasis has been laid upon Jesus as ' The Man of Sorrows,' that too often we have forgotten how His life and teaching radiated joy. He spoke of His disciples as ' sons of the bride-chamber.' Again and again he bade men ' Be of good cheer.' He spoke of joy as the reward of fidelity. ' Enter thou into the joy of thy lord.' He told His followers to rejoice when they were persecuted. Even in the farewell of the upper room, with the stark shadow of the Cross enfolding Him, Jesus spoke of His joy, that should be transmitted to the lonely disciples.

The early Church had discovered how wondrously Jesus was fulfilling that promise. One of the strikingly dominant notes of the book of the Acts of the Apostles is its joy. There is little of the minor and much of the major. In an age of sterile and torturing despair, ' they began to be merry.' So hilarious were they on the day of Pentecost, that they had the abandon of intoxicated men, and some of the bystanders were misled.

> Bliss was it in that dawn to be alive,
> And to be young was very heaven.

And the joy of that amazing day was no transient emotion, born but to die when confronted with the morrow's grey dawn. These early Christians found new radiance in the common ways of life, and their joy bubbled forth in their daily tasks. Even their meals were mirthful—' they ate their bread with gladness.' (Those who have been in any fellowship at Swanwick will appreciate this sidelight upon the life of the first followers of the Way.)

They could withstand and even defeat persecution. How can you overcome men who run away after a flogging with the high spirits of schoolboys at the end of term ? 'And when they had called the apostles unto them, they beat them and charged them not to speak in the name of Jesus, and let them go. They therefore departed from the presence of the council, rejoicing that they were counted worthy to suffer dishonour for the Name ' (Acts v. 40, 41). How can you silence men like Paul and Silas, who could sing even at midnight in a stuffy prison with their backs bruised and bleeding and their feet fast in the stocks ? As Dr. Glover says : ' With "the sentence of death in themselves," the early Christians faced the world and astonished it by more than their " stubbornness." They were the most essentially happy people of the day. Jesus was their hope, their sufficiency was of God, their names were written in heaven, they were full of love for all men—they had " become little children," as Jesus put it, glad and natural.'

And that experience of joy has been the rich possession of God's children in all ages. Let John Nelson (one of Wesley's preachers) bear his testimony. To prevent his preaching he was seized by a press gang for the army, and flung into a dungeon in Bradford. 'But,' he writes in his *Journal*, 'my Master never sends His servants a warfare at their own charge : He gives strength according to their day. For, when I came into the dungeon, that stunk worse than a hog-stye by reason of the blood and filth which sink from the butchers who kill over it, my soul was so filled with the love of God, that it was a paradise to me.

'Then could I cry out, "O the glorious liberty of the sons of God!" And I fell down on my knees, and gave God thanks, that He counted me worthy to be put into a dungeon for the truth's sake; and prayed that my enemies might be saved from the wrath to come, I think with as much desire as I could feel for my mother's own children. I wished they were as happy in their own houses, as I was in the dungeon.

'About ten, several of the people came to the dungeon-door, and brought me some candles, and put me some meat and water in through the hole of the door. When I had eaten and drunk, I gave God thanks, and we sang hymns almost all night, they without and I within.'

John Haime, another of Wesley's preachers, can bear the same glorious witness. He was a dragoon at Dettingen in 1743, and writes: 'The battle was soon joined with small arms as well as cannon, on both sides. It was very bloody: thousands, on each side, were sent to their long home. I had no sooner joined the regiment than my left-hand man was shot dead. I cried to God, and said, "In Thee have I trusted, let me never be confounded." My heart was filled with love, joy, and peace, more than tongue can express. I was in a new world. I could truly say, "Unto you that believe He is precious."'

Yet another, George Shadford, gives his glowing testimony: 'As I walked home along the streets, I seemed to be in paradise. When I read my Bible, it seemed an entirely new book. When I meditated on God and Christ, angels or spirits ; when I considered good or bad men, any or all the creatures which surrounded me on every side ; everything appeared new, and stood in a new relation to me. I was in Christ a new creature ; old things were done away, and all things become new. I lay down at night in peace with a thankful heart, because the Lord had redeemed me, and given me peace with God and all mankind. . . . I felt the truth of those words—

On the wings of His love
I was carried above
All sin, and temptation, and pain ;
I could not believe
I ever should grieve,
I ever should suffer again.

' I was happy, happy in my God ; clothed with the sun, and the moon under my feet ; raised up, and made to sit in heavenly, holy, happy places in Christ Jesus.'

Frances Ridley Havergal found the joy of this experience. Her religion made her bright, cheerful, and radiant. A schoolfellow said of her, that she was ' like a bird flashing into the room, her fair sunny curls falling round her shoulders, her bright eyes dancing, and her fresh sweet voice ringing through the room.' She once heard a hymn-singing party described as ' religiously jolly,' and wrote, ' The expression by no means displeased me, because it is just what I wish, to get people to connect religion with all that is pleasant and joyful.'

She was of the same mind as Charles Wesley, who asks

> Who hath a right like us to sing,
>   Us, whom His mercy raises ?
> Merry our hearts, for Christ is King,
>   Cheerful are all our faces.

The converted Japanese, Kanso Utschimura, swells the chorus : ' My friends soon noted my changed mood. Formerly, as soon as I came in sight of the temple, I was dumb, for I had to say my prayers in my heart. Now, I chattered and laughed joyously all the way to college. . . . Belief in one God made me a new man.'

From India comes Sadhu Sundar Singh's witness : ' I remember the night when I was driven out of my home—the first night. When I came to know my Saviour I told my father and my brother and my other relations. At first they did not take much notice ; but afterwards they thought that it was a great dishonour that I should become a Christian, and so I was driven out of my home. The first night I had to spend in cold weather under a tree. I had had no such experience. I was not used to living in such a place without a shelter. I began to think : " Yesterday and before that I used to live in the midst of luxury at my home ; but now I am shivering here, and hungry and thirsty and without shelter, with no warm clothes and no food." I had to spend the whole night under the tree But I remember the wonderful joy and peace in my heart, the presence of my Saviour. I held my New Testament in my hand. I remember that first night as my first night in heaven I remember the wonderful joy that made me compare that time with the time when I was living in a luxurious home. In the midst of luxuries and comfort I could not find peace in my heart. The presence of the Saviour changed the suffering into peace.'

George Fox tells the same story : ' My troubles continued and I was often under great temptations. I fasted much, walked abroad in solitary places many days, and often took my Bible and sat in hollow trees and lonesome places till night came on, and frequently in the night walked about by myself. . . . When all my hopes in all men were gone so that I had nothing outwardly to help me, nor could I tell what to do, then, O then, I heard a Voice which said, "There is one even Christ Jesus, that can speak to thy condition." When I heard it, my heart did leap for joy.'

Two moderns, members of the Cambridge Group, put it in fresh and delightfully unconventional language :

' When I came away, things had taken on a " radiance " (it's the only word I can think of)— and that has lasted ever since. It may seem a bit soon to start shouting about things. But I feel quite sure in my own mind that I've got something new, permanently.' The second testifies, ' I got the " bubbly " feeling, and it won't go.'

These all, men and women, ancient and modern, bear their witness to the truth which centuries ago Paul discovered, ' The fruit of the Spirit is . . . joy.'

DAILY READINGS

1. Matthew xxv. 14-23.
2. 1 Peter i. 1-12.
3. Acts ii. 46 ; v. 41 ; xvi. 25.
4. Acts xi. 23 ; 2 John 4 ; 3 John 3, 4.
5. Ephesians v. 8-20.
6. 2 Corinthians vii. 3-16.

QUESTIONARY

1. Bill Brewer says ' Christians are nothing but " kill-joys." Make him discuss this.
2. Take any hymn of thanksgiving and read it carefully. Compare the reasons for thankfulness given there with those that you usually remember.
3. Wordsworth declared that he wished to ' Keep the sprightly soul awake.' How would you do that ?

THE POWER OF THE TRANSFORMING EXPERIENCE

C

III

THE POWER OF THE TRANSFORMING
EXPERIENCE

IN considering the courage that is born of the transforming experience, we may well recall the instance of the eleven disciples. Before Pentecost they had shown themselves a prey to panic. All of them had fled when their Master was arrested in dark Gethsemane. Peter, despite all his protestations of devotion and bravery, had quailed before the questioning of a maidservant. After the hours of the Crucifixion, when they met together, the doors were shut fast, 'for fear of the Jews.' The original manuscript of St. Mark's gospel closes with a sombre picture of terrified women (Mark xvi, 8), 'for they were afraid.'

But after the transforming experience of Pentecost, the glow of their strangely warmed hearts put all fears to flight. We see a new Peter. He who but a few brief weeks before had been a shrinking craven was changed into a fearless stalwart. It was the BOLDNESS of Peter and John that compelled the Sanhedrin to recognize that these 'uncultured persons and mere outsiders' had been the companions of Jesus, of whose courage, even unto death, they had been made well aware. Before their new experience the disciples and the handful of believers had huddled behind closed doors, now they came out boldly to give their ringing testimony in the face of excited and prejudiced throngs, who crowded Jerusalem from many a distant town and village. Just ' outside the city wall ' was grim Golgotha, and Peter knew of a surety that he was inviting imprisonment and scourging and even death, when he declared that Jesus had been crucified by the hands of lawless men, and ended with the poignant home thrust, ' You have crucified your own Messiah.'

Think of the shining courage of Ananias of Damascus in going to the house of Judas to inquire for Saul of Tarsus, who had set out for the express purpose of haling him and his fellow Christians to prison and to death. He had none of the encouragement that comradeship in adventure gives, so far as human companions went, but Jesus was with him, and secure in the knowledge that the strong Son of God was by his side, he bravely faced the unknown.

Edmund Burke said of himself, ' I was not rocked and swaddled and dandled into a legislator. " Nitor in adversum," is the motto for a man like you.' That was a motto which the early Church might well have adopted for its own, so truly does it express their spirit. They were indeed believers fighting and watching. They passed triumphantly and fearlessly through ' great doors and effectual,' though they knew full well that behind those doors ' many adversaries ' envenomed and watchful, lay in wait. The New Testament writings plainly show that to follow Jesus was hazardous and costly. They ' endured a great conflict of sufferings ; partly, being made a gazing-stock both by reproaches and afflictions ; and partly, becoming partakers with them that were so used.'

They 'took joyfully the spoiling of their possessions' (Heb. x. 32–34). The world hated them
(1 John iii. 13). Jason, Aquila and Priscilla, Gaius
and Aristarchus, the Churches at Thessalonica and
Philippi, as well as Stephen, Paul, Peter, James,
and John knew what it was to suffer for their Lord.

As Bishop Westcott has reminded us : ' Heathenism
was so mixed up with the ordinary routine of society
and home that the believer would be forced to stand
in a position of continual protest. The proceedings
of the courts, the public ceremonies, the ordinary
amusements, were more or less connected with
idolatrous forms and observances. The smoking
altar constantly called for some sign of abhorrence.
The universal presence of the images of the gods made
watchful caution a necessity for the believer. The
common language of familiar conversation often
required a disclaimer of the superstition on which
it was framed. . . . Under such circumstances the
Christian could not but be brought frequently into
direct opposition to the popular faith, however
carefully he might avoid positions of danger, and
however liberally he might interpret the law of charity.
The cases might be rare where the conscript refused
to serve in the army or accept the badge of his
enlistment, where the soldier refused to imitate his
comrades in wearing the crown which he interpreted
as the symbol of slavery to a heathen power, where
the yearly banquet on the emperor's birthday stirred
the conscience of the centurion and moved him to
cast off the symbol of his profession ; but these kept
the idea of the conflict present to the minds of men
and invested the smaller divergences in thought

and conduct with their real importance. In this way Christianity challenged persecution.'

But none of these things could move them. They were steadfast, unmovable, always abounding in the work of the Lord. They had learned the secret of courage, that they could do all things through the strength of Christ. Dungeon, stripes, exile, wild beasts, could not affright them. They had a mystic power that gave them patience to endure and courage even in the darkest hour. And this spirit has persisted all down the long corridor of the centuries. The martyr roll of the Church is long and varied. The noble army of martyrs includes ' men and boys, the matron and the maid.'

The early Methodists demonstrated the power of the new experience. They faced murderous mobs, they were assailed and abused, but they triumphed over their troubles. Their story should never be allowed to die, for it reveals the courage given by their Captain, Christ. Wesley has left on record his experience of the Walsall mob. They beset him with angry cries, like the roaring of the sea, madly yelling, ' Knock his brains out ; down with him ; kill him at once.' He was roughly dragged by his hair, and thrust mercilessly along from one end of the town to the other. But he can write, ' From the beginning to the end I found the same presence of mind, as if I had been sitting in my own study.' And that spirit was shared by the loyal, simple Methodists who refused to desert him in his peril.

' It ought not to be forgotten,' he writes, ' that when the rest of the society made all haste to escape for their lives, four only would not stir, William Sitch,

Edward Slater, John Griffiths, and Joan Parks ; these kept with me, resolving to live or die together ; and none of them received one blow, but William Sitch, who held me by the arm, from one end of the town to the other. He was then dragged away and knocked down ; but he soon rose and got to me again. I afterwards asked him, what he expected when the mob came upon us. He said, " To die for Him who had died for me " ; and he felt no hurry or fear. . . . I asked J. Parks if she was not afraid, when they tore her from me. She said, " No ; no more than I am now. I could trust God for you, as well as for myself." '

And that preserving and sustaining power has been manifested not only in situations of grave peril, but also in the more common tests of our daily life. When men and women have been strengthened by the Spirit's power penetrating to the very roots of their being, they have been enabled to meet difficulties and to launch out upon adventures from which, before the new experience came, they would have shrunk in dread and dismay. When there comes the thrilling and empowering sense of the sustaining presence of Jesus, men no longer feebly excuse themselves and cry, ' I can't,' or more honestly, ' I won't.' Their sufficiency is of God, and their glad and eager response to the challenge of the hour is ' Here am I, send me.'

The distressing and perplexing problem of the present dearth of Christian workers, and the impoverishment and lack of élan in so much of our Church life, would be immediately solved by the glowing experience of the presence of Jesus, whose Name ' charms our fears.'

Captain Hadfield has thus summarized the New Testament experience : ' No reader of the New Testament can fail to be struck by the constant reiteration in different forms of the idea that the normal experience of a Christian at that epoch was enhancement of power—" I can do all things "—an enhancement attributed by them to the operation in and through them of a divine energy to which the community gave the name of the " Spirit." . . . Pentecost, the healing miracles of the Apostolic Age, the triumphant progress of the religion through the Roman Empire, the heroic deeds of saints and martyrs—all these point to a sense of power newly discovered. In contrast, looking at the Church of to-day, one cannot but be struck with its powerlessness. It contains men of intellect ; it produces a type of piety and devotion which one cannot but admire ; it sacrifices itself in works of kindness and beneficence ; but even its best friends would not claim that it inspires in the world a sense of power. What strikes one rather is its impotence and failure. This want of inspiration and power is associated with the fact that men no longer believe in the existence of the Spirit in any effective practical way. They believe in God the Father, and they are reverent ; they believe in the Son, and the Church numbers among its members millions who humbly try to " follow in His steps " ; but for all practical purposes they are like that little band at Ephesus who had " not so much as heard whether there be any Holy Ghost," and, lacking the inspiration of such a belief, they are weak and wonder why.'

DAILY READINGS

1. Mark xiv. 50-72.
2. Acts ii. 14-36.
3. Acts xiii. 42-52.
4. Rev. vii. 9-17.
5. 2 Cor. xii. 1-10.
6. Philippians iv. 10-20.

QUESTIONARY

1. Swinburne wrote of ' the lilies and languors of virtue.'
   Correct him.
2. How can we find ' a moral equivalent for war ' ?
3. ' Hold the fort for I am coming.'
   Is that the truth ?

THE DELIVERANCE BROUGHT BY THE NEW EXPERIENCE

IV

THE DELIVERANCE BROUGHT BY THE NEW
EXPERIENCE

THE new experience has always brought a glorious sense of liberty and release. We have already noted the deliverance from fear and weakness that it brought, but the scope of the new freedom was far wider and richer. Men found forgiveness. ' The old sense of being in the wrong with God is gone, and God has not one word of condemnation now for those who are united with Jesus Christ ' (Rom. viii. 1). The first believers found salvation from sin. They were designated saints, a title which we nowadays shrink from and regard with a measure of suspicion. As the Rev. A. J. Gossip has reminded us: ' Even that healthy-minded man of genius, Neil Munro, stumbles into some silly chatter in his *Fancy Farm*, " No saint, remember ; saints are for the most part women, invalids, and elders." '

Jesus had declared ' By their fruits ye shall know them,' and the fruits of the new experience are seen in moral transformation. Paul can appeal to his ' living letters.' His converts were ' dead to sin.' He gives a long, black catalogue of victims of vice, and then adds in tones of ringing triumph, ' And such were some of you, but ye were washed, but ye were sanctified, but ye were justified in the name of the Lord Jesus Christ, and in the Spirit of our God.'

This, too, is a timeless note of the new and transforming experience. Mark Rutherford wrote : ' I

45

can assure my incredulous literary friends that years ago it was not uncommon for men and women suddenly to wake up to the fact that they had been sinners, and to affirm that henceforth they would keep God's commandments by the help of Jesus Christ and the Holy Spirit. What is more extraordinary is that they did keep God's commandments for the rest of their lives.'

The evil chains of habit have been triumphantly snapped, the taints of heredity have been overcome, the deadly grip of debasing environment has been mastered. Mr. W. E. H. Lecky has recognized this, for he wrote : ' It was reserved for Christianity to present to the world an ideal character which, through all the changes of eighteen centuries, has filled the hearts of men with an impassioned love, and has shown itself capable of acting on all ages, nations, temperaments and conditions ; has not only been the highest pattern of virtue, but the highest incentive to its practice, and has exerted so deep an influence that it may be truly said that the simple record of three short years of active life has done more to regenerate and to soften mankind than all the disquisitions of philosophers, and than all the exhortations of moralists. This has indeed been the wellspring of whatever has been best and purest in the Christian life. Amid all the sins and failings, amid all the priestcraft, the persecution and fanaticism which have defaced the Church, it has preserved in the character and example of its Founder an enduring principle of regeneration.'

Dr. W. L. Northridge in his *Recent Psychology and Evangelistic Preaching* adduces modern instances that have come within his own observation, of the deliverance from sin effected by the converting power of the gospel. Mr. H—— was a slave to drink, unreliable, mean and cruel in his treatment of his wife and children. After his conversion, he declared, ' All the old feelings and cravings had disappeared, and others, altogether new to me, took possession of my heart.' And Dr. Northridge adds this testimony : ' This remarkable change of inner feeling and thought has manifested itself in a changed life. For straightforwardness, strength of will, gentleness of disposition, sympathy with those in need, and tenderness of heart, Mr. H—— is, in the judgement of the writer, unrivalled.'

Mr. B—— was a hard and selfish gambler, cynical, and critical of all religion. After the transforming experience became his, ' Not only did his selfishness disappear, but his harsh, cynical, and dour spirit as well. A tenderness of nature seldom surpassed henceforth characterized his life and manifested itself in all sorts of ways.'

Mr. P—— indulged in the grossest forms of sin for over forty years, but, ' It is difficult for any one who knows Mr. P—— as he now is to imagine that he could ever have lived the life of indifference, self-indulgence, and recklessness at which we have only hinted. He tells of the new feelings and desires that his conversion has resulted in, of the complete disappearance of all evil tendencies, of the breaking of ingrained habits, and of the experience of a completely new set of impulses His love for little children, his pity for those who are the slaves of vices from which he has been set free, his anxiety to have restored to him

" the years that the locust hath eaten," by henceforth making the most of his life—all prove unmistakably that a new life of singular beauty and tenderness has, through faith in Christ, come into being.'

I heard a man, a Christian worker for many years, bravely tell what the new and transforming experience had meant to him. He found a living God, and that new sense brought him deliverance. For years he had been the victim of an evil habit, but the realization of God brought cleansing ; ' I felt as if I had been cleaned by a disinfectant sponge,' were his words.

And, lest any should critically cry, ' These are extreme instances, but what of so-called Christian people who are touchy, narrow, proud, ill-tempered, gossipy, and malicious ? ' let Miriam Gray give her testimony : ' Truly I don't have to bother myself much about my temper now, and honestly I don't think anybody else does either. But it isn't because I have got a new and stronger chain for the beast ; rather it has become God's beast, as everything I am and have has become God's. And so when the stress of life bears hard, and stupidities— my own and other people's—vex my tired and irritable nerves (and they are horribly irritable, I can tell you), why, He is there—not only His touch, His look : more, His very self—and irritation, like fear, dies before Him. *He is always enough.*'

John Newton wrote his own epitaph that he, being dead, might testify to the great deliverance which he had experienced :

JOHN NEWTON, Clerk
Once an infidel and libertine,
A servant of slaves in Africa :
Was by the rich mercy of our Lord and Saviour
Jesus Christ,
Preserved, restored, pardoned,
And appointed to preach the Faith
He had long laboured to destroy.
Near sixteen years at Olney in Bucks :
And twenty-seven years in this Church.

And that is the true harvest of the transforming experience. The sense of sin is deepened, but the knowledge of the love of God and of the help of the ever present Saviour is so intensified, that there is newness of life. The experience is ethical. That is the acid test of its reality. Restitution is made, long-standing feuds are forgotten, there is a new appreciation of the meaning of duty, there is a moral deliverance.

As Dr. Simon has written, ' " The remission of sins " : that is the trumpet note that sounds clearly through the morning air of every great revival.' To struggling men and women the new experience brings glad knowledge of forgiveness for the bitter past, power for the tests of the present, and joyous assurance for the future, all unknown.

It brings deliverance from doubt and fear. It is significant that in the Book of Acts, one of the most frequent designations of the members of the early Church was ' Believers,' or a cognate word. ' All that believed were together ' (Acts ii. 44). ' And the multitude of them that believed were of one heart and soul ' (Acts iv. 32). ' And there were the more added to them, believing on the Lord ' (Acts v. 14).

Apollos, at Corinth, ' helped them much which had

believed through grace ' (Acts xviii. 27). Moreover, this faith was not blind, but remarkably intelligent. They stressed repentance. Too often we debase this rich word, and associate it merely with the maudlin and sentimental. But its root meaning is ' change of mind,' and the early Christian not only repented in the sense that he was sincerely and deeply sorry for his past sinfulness, but also in the sense that he began to think. He was a free thinker of the right school. He was willing to scrap his old theories, to forget all prejudices, to seek for truth at all costs. To quote Dr Glover : ' The Christian read the best books, assimilated them, and lived the freest intellectual life that the world had. . . . Who did the thinking in that ancient world ? Again and again it was the Christian. He out-thought the world.'

Paul is the outstanding example of this. A stalwart of the Moses Bible Union, he appeared to have a hermetically sealed mind. But when Jesus came with compelling force into his life, he was forced to think. He thought in the darkness of those days of blindness in the house of Judas in Damascus. He went away to brood in the Arabian solitudes, and he came back with a new gospel, a message that was his own, born of thought and prayer and hallowed communion with the great Teacher.

The new experience brings deliverance from all that is dry and formal. In the Parable of the Good Samaritan Jesus showed how grieviously the religious leaders of His day had divorced worship from practical service. The new Church was no longer enslaved by sapless and barren creeds, but had its living message for the street as well as for the synagogue, for the worker as well as for the worshipper.

DAILY READINGS

1. Romans vi. 1-6.
2. 1 Corinthians vi. 9-20.
3. Hebrews x. 32-39.
4. Romans viii. 1-11.
5. 1 Peter i. 17-25.
6. 1 John iii. 1-8.

QUESTIONARY

1. What do we really mean by ' salvation ? '
2. How would you help a prisoner to escape from a twentieth-century Doubting Castle ?
3. How would you translate ' Saving Faith ' in terms of the present age ?

THE TRANSMISSION OF THE NEW
EXPERIENCE

V

THE TRANSMISSION OF THE NEW EXPERIENCE.

THE story of the Acts of the Apostles bears vivid and impressive witness to the transmission of the transforming experience of God in Jesus Christ. It is a record of the sustained and vigorous growth of the infant Church and the contagion of its new and thrilling life. At the dawn of the day of Pentecost the followers of the ' Way ' numbered but a few score, and to the outward observer the prospect of its success, or even of its existence, must have appeared to be but pitifully poor. Yet ere that memorable day drew to its close, thousands had been added to its joyful membership.

The records show that this was no transient success, begotten of a merely ephemeral emotion, for we read that the number of those who believed was increased ' day by day.' On Paul's arrival at Jerusalem for what proved to be his last visit, James and the elders could cry exultantly, ' Thou seest, brother, how many myriads (R. V. margin) there are among the Jews which have believed,' (Acts xxi. 20). Paul could write to the Christians of Colossae that the gospel ' spreads over all the world with fruit and increase, (Col. i. 16, Moffatt's translation).

The early Church speedily showed itself an aggressive Church. The experience of Pentecost did not detain those who shared it within the four walls of their upper room, nursing their ecstasy or debating its validity. It drove them forth to witness in the open air, amongst the hostile Samaritans, and to missionary enterprise in Gentile fields. Filled with the Holy Spirit, they were filled with holy energy, and their gospel became rapidly diffused. They had enjoyed an experience of God which they not only could, but must, transmit to others. The flowing tide swept them gloriously along.

> My heart is full of Christ, and longs
>   Its glorious matter to declare.
> Of Him I make my loftier songs,
>   I cannot from His praise forbear ;
> My ready tongue makes haste to sing
> The glories of my heavenly King.

That was the experience of the believer who had willingly become the captive of Christ.

Sir W. M. Ramsay has thus described the growth and development of the Apostolic Church : ' The Church was not inactive for a day after the coming of the Spirit of Pentecost. It was constantly exerting itself both in external growth through the preaching of the Word, and in internal development through the improvement of its administration and the organization of charity. So Luke's history, when rightly understood, is fatal to that fashionable modern theory which regards the early Christians as simply waiting in expectation of the immediate coming of Jesus Christ to reign upon the earth. The confidence in the Kingdom of God which they felt was not a feeling that made them sit inactive ; it roused them to strenuous activity and preparation. Every one was at work, each in his own way ; Peter the leader, yet always ready to learn from the bolder initiative of others like Stephen and Philip. Each attempt to muzzle or suppress the new faith only resulted in increasing the energy and widening the range of missionary effort.' They won successes even in the most unlikely fields. For a Jew to win converts in Samaria, as Philip did, was to achieve the miraculous, for the estrangement of Jew and Samaritan was proverbial. St. John has reminded us of the true position, Jews have no dealings with Samaritans. But Jesus had bidden His followers bear their witness even in the most unlikely field ' in Samaria,' and full of confidence and power, they journeyed forth to achieve the impossible. They measured their tasks by the standard of Christ who was within them the hope of glory.

Jesus had been strangely moved when the little deputation of Greeks had desired to see Him on the eve of Calvary. He plainly regarded their approach on such an errand as the pledge of the glory of the coming ingathering. He was about to die, but His death would bear much fruit, and He, lifted up from the earth, would draw all men to Him. The book of the Acts of the Apostles records the glowing story of the beginning of the harvest. Greek and Roman accepted Jesus as Lord. In Pisidian Antioch, Iconium, Lystra, Derbe, Syrian Antioch, Philippi, Thessalonica, Berea, Corinth, Ephesus, Colossae, Laodicea, Smyrna, Pergamum, Thyatira, Sardis, and Philadelphia—and even in cities like Athens and

Rome—converts were won. Facing frenzied mobs, battling with obstinate superstition and ingrained bigotry, the heralds of the Cross went forth to pull down these strongholds of sin and Satan, ' more than conquerors ' to use Paul's exuberant words.

Many of the converts were men and women of rank, wealth, and culture. They included the Ethiopian chancellor, Sergius Paulus, the pro-consul of Cyprus, Barnabas, Lydia, Cornelius, Manaen, ' of the chief women ' in Thessalonica ' not a few,' and in Berea ' of the Greek women of honourable estate, and of men, not a few.'

Saul of Tarsus, the most notable convert, was a university man, and there is reason to believe that he was by no means poor. Felix certainly believed that he was possessed of the means to secure his freedom by bribery—' he hoped withal that money would be given him of Paul.' Luke was a doctor, and—so tradition avers—an artist. Remembering the difficulties experienced in India in winning over those of high caste, we can more readily realize the deep significance of the tremendous triumphs of grace in the first century.

This success was gained by what may well be termed ' team-work.' It is true that Peter and Paul were the outstanding figures, towering like Titans above the rest, but their gifts and energies were supplemented and extended by a great host of humble but ardent workers. The apostles remained in Jerusalem when persecution followed the martyrdom of Stephen, but the scattered rank and file went forth with hearts aflame to proclaim their joyful news.

Gibbon declared that the primary cause of the

amazing diffusion of the new religion lay in the fact that ' it became the most sacred duty of a new convert to diffuse among his friends the inestimable blessing which he had received.'

Harnack's testimony is equally clear and emphatic: ' We cannot hesitate to believe that the great mission of Christianity was in reality accomplished by means of informal missionaries.'

Aquila and Priscilla, humble tent-makers, help the cultured and eloquent Apollos to a more perfect understanding of the way of life. Paul could write of Phoebe — otherwise unknown — that she had been a succourer of many ; of Persis, that she had laboured much in the Lord, and of the rest of my fellow labourers whose names are in the book of life.

The young Pliny, when pro-consul of Bithynia and Pontus, in a famous letter to the Emperor, stated that Christianity had spread throughout his province, not only in the cities, but also in the villages and rural areas, that the pagan rites were being inter-rupted, and that the temples were almost deserted. The true significance of this is fully realized only when we recall the statement of Acts xvi. 7, that Paul and Timothy ' assayed to go into Bithynia ; and the Spirit of Jesus suffered them not.' The work left unaccomplished by them because they were being led on to the great fields of Europe, was achieved by some unsung evangelists.

A young woman in Jamaica recently cried in her prayer, ' Lord, I cannot hold very much, but I can do a lot of overflowing.' The transforming experience compels men and women to ' do a lot of overflowing.'

There is no other way for them.   The love of Christ constrains.

O let me commend my Saviour to you,

is the glad utterance of those who feel the presence of Jesus.

Let Wesley's preachers testify. John Pawson writes : ' Having found salvation myself, I felt an intense desire that others should enjoy the same blessing.'

Sampson Staniforth was won by a fellow soldier, Mark Bond, concerning whom he writes : ' At the beginning of the campaign, he went to hear the preaching of John Haime, William Clements, and John Evans.   There he found what he wanted.   God soon spake peace to his soul, and he rejoiced with joy unspeakable. He then began to think whom he should open his mind to. He thought of several ; but could fix on none but me. He could not shake me off his mind, till he came to me and told me what God had done for his soul, adding, how desperate my case would be if I died without experiencing the same. . . . He came to me after, but I would not hear him. He then endeavoured to turn his thoughts on someone else ; but I was continually on his mind, sleeping and waking. He could not rest, either day or night, but it was on his mind, " Go to Sampson." He came to me and told me what he had felt and suffered on my account. But I did not mind it, till he met me one time, when I was in distress, having neither food, money, nor credit. On his coming and asking me to go and hear the preaching, I said, " You had better give me something to eat or drink ; for I

I am both hungry and dry.'' He took me to a sutler's and gave me both meat and drink. Then he took me by the hand, and led to me a place erected about half a mile from the camp. I had no desire to hear anything of religion, but on the contrary went with great reluctance. Who it was that was speaking, I do not know ; but I know this, that God spake to my heart. In a few minutes I was in deep distress, full of sorrow, under a deep sense of sin and danger, but mixed with a desire of mercy. And now, I that never prayed in my life, was continually calling upon God : in time past, I could shed tears for nothing ; but now the rock was rent ; a fountain was opened, and tears of contrition ran plentifully down my cheeks. A cry after God was put into my heart, which has never yet ceased, and, I trust, never will. My dear companion observed it with great joy . . . When the preaching was over, my dear companion took me in his arms, and blessed God with a joyful heart.'

Thomas Hanson writes : ' On July 16, at night, 1757, under my brother Joseph's prayer, I yielded, sunk, and as it were, died away. My heart with a kind, sweet struggle, melted into the hands of God. I was for some hours lost in wonder, by the astonishing peace, love, and joy which flowed into my heart like a mighty torrent . . . From this night I could not hold my tongue from speaking of the things of God.'

John Nelson bears the same witness : ' In the time of my convictions, I never let my wife know of my trouble ; but now I could not eat my morsel alone. I therefore wrote to her and all my relations, to seek the same mercy that I had found.'

Billy Bray in the last century, feels the same urge : ' When I was converted, praise the Lord, He gave me strength to tell all I met with, that I was happy, and that what the Lord had done for me He would do for anybody else that would seek His face.'

The Christian Crusade waits not for appointed times and seasons. ' *Now* is the accepted time, *now* is the day of salvation,' was Paul's message, not to sinners, but to Church members.

' One loving heart sets another on fire.' That was how the disciple group was first founded and then enlarged. Andrew findeth Peter ; Philip aflame runs to tell Nathanael, and jerks out his words in his eagerness ; ' the Samaritans believed in Him because of the word of the woman ' ; men healed and restored, ' spread it abroad.'

The transforming experience not only can be shared, but it must be shared. It cannot be hid. The cup runs over.

> What we have felt and seen,
> With confidence we tell.

DAILY READINGS

1. Acts ii. 41, 47 ; iv. 4 ; v. 14 ; vi. 7 ; ix. 31.
2. Acts viii. 4-8.
3. Acts xi. 19-26.
4. Acts viii. 26-39.
5. Acts xviii. 26 ; 1 Thess. i. 8-10.
6. 1 Cor. vi. 9-11 ; 2 Cor. v. 17, 18.

QUESTIONARY

1. Collect all the references you can find to Aquila and Priscilla, and, remembering that they were two ordinary business people, discuss how they would act to-day in your Church.
2. What is a successful ' mission ' ?
3. If an ' outsider ' was found in your pew, what would you do ?

FELLOWSHIP AND THE NEW EXPERIENCE

VI

FELLOWSHIP AND THE NEW EXPERIENCE

'THE gospel,' wrote Harnack, 'spiritualizes the irresistible impulse which draws one man to another.' The 'corporate spirit' was one of the most distinctive features of the life of the early Church. Yet it must not be forgotten that the nucleus of that Church—the first band of twelve disciples of Jesus—had not found it easy to learn the team spirit. The gospel portraiture is unsparing in its delineation of their faults as well as of their virtues. We find that very often—to the grief of their Master—they showed themselves, self-seeking, jealous, touchy, quarrelsome and opinionated. Yet, living in close and intimate fellowship with Jesus, catching the charm of His fragrant spirit, seeing daily His acts of unselfishness and love, crowned by the final surrender of all that He had on the cruel cross with its pain and shame, they became new men, their characters were wondrously transformed, and, little by little, the old things passed away. They began to look at truth with new eyes, to be ready to 'give and take.' They became dearer to each other and less and less self-regarding as their risen and living Friend became dearer and more precious to each of them. 'They had all things common,' and 'all things' implies much more than mere possessions.

Jesus had promised that those who obeyed His silver call and followed Him should find new spiritual affinities and a larger and richer family life in exchange for those left behind for His sake (Mark x. 30), and they found that this promise, like every other of His, was abundantly fulfilled. Paul could write to the Christians of Rome, ' So, too, for all our numbers, we form one Body in Christ, and we are severally members one of another' (Rom. xii. 5). He had left his home in Tarsus, and been estranged from his kith and kin for the sake of the gospel, but he had found another mother in the mother of Rufus. (Rom. xvi. 13.) (If the Rufus he mentions is the son of Simon of Cyrene, and if Simon of Cyrene is to be identified with Simeon who was called Niger—The Black—Simon and his wife may well have been native Africans. This is, of course, purely conjectural, but, if correct, it opens fruitful avenues of thought to regard Paul as calling a native African woman his ' Mother.' Here would be true fellowship of a kind so dear to the apostle's heart, that leaped triumphantly over the sundering ' colour bar.')

Sir W. M. Ramsay has well written : ' The principle was established that all parts and members of the Universal Church should help to support and stimulate the life of each other. The practical working out of this principle involved constant intercourse between separate parts of the Church, the transmission of knowledge to all parts about everything that concerned every part, the interchange of ideas, the sending of letters, the travelling of individuals from congregation to congregation, the hospitable reception of every traveller wherever he went, the sense of

unity and brotherhood brought home to every
traveller by finding in all cities Christian friends
believing and thinking like himself. This constant
inter-communication was of inestimable importance ;
it was the circulation of the very life-blood of the
Church.'

The early Church soon learned the lesson of fellowship. Pentecost was the fruit of earnest, patient,
prayerful and united waiting upon God. In the one
hundred and twenty gathered together there were
varying types. Men knelt beside women. Peter
the impetuous learned from Thomas the cautious.
Simon the revolutionary could find strange unity
with Matthew the ex-civil servant. Beginners like
the brethren of Jesus sat with humble and teachable
minds at the feet of those who had companied with
Him and were more advanced in His wondrous school.
There were ' Churches ' in the houses of the first
believers. Men and women came together impelled
by a common sense of need and a common love of
Jesus, and in Christian society were comforted and
instructed by each other's varying experiences, and
were thereby strengthened to pursue the heavenward
way. Dr Anderson Scott suggests that the true
meaning of ' the fellowship of the Holy Spirit ' is the
fellowship which the Holy Spirit creates and sustains.
The early Church did not forget that their Lord had
set about the tremendous task of saving a lost world
by forming a group of twelve, that they might be
with Him. They regarded the Church as a family,
a brotherhood. (1 Peter ii. 17.) Right through the
amazing story of the Acts of the Apostles we read
of ' the brethren,' from its opening (i. 15), to its

close. (xxviii. 15.) ' Love of the brethren was a well-marked characteristic of their new corporate life.'

Bunyan, in his day, knew the value of true fellow-ship. Well might he, for it was the transforming experience uttered by a few simple women who were sitting in the sun in a street in Bedford, that gave him an insight into the excellence and joy of true and heart-felt personal knowledge of God. He himself was a ' brisk talker ' (and unhappily the race is by no means extinct !) but theirs was a real and convincing experience. He says :

' Their talk was about a new birth, the work of God in their hearts, as also how they were convinced of their miserable state by nature. They talked how God had visited their souls with His love in the Lord Jesus, and with what words and promises they had been refreshed, comforted and supported against the temptations of the devil. Moreover, they reasoned of the suggestions and temptations of Satan in particular, and told each other by what means they had been afflicted, and how they were borne up under his assaults. They also discoursed of their own wretchedness of heart, and of their unbelief, and did contemn, slight, and abhor their own righteousness as filthy, and insufficient to do them any good. And methought they spake with such pleasantness of Scripture language, and with such appearance of grace in all they said, that they were to me as if they had found a new world. . . . Therefore I would often make it my business to be going again and again into the company of these poor people, for I could not stay away ; and the more I went among them, the more did I question my condition.'

In the Valley of the Shadow of Death Christian was cheered by the glad discovery that he was not alone in that noisome and dangerous place, but, hearing the voice of Faithful, rejoiced, even there, to find fellowship. When Faithful was martyred, Hopeful became Christian's fellow-pilgrim, and their fellowship proved fruitful on the drowsy levels of the Enchanted Ground. Christian's song was Bunyan's own experience :

> When saints do sleepy grow, let them come hither
> And hear how these two pilgrims talk together ;
> Yea, let them learn of them in any wise
> Thus to keep ope their drowsy, slumb'ring eyes.
> Saints' fellowship, if it be managed well,
> Keeps them awake, and that in spite of hell.

Wesley knew the value of experimental fellowship, for it was in a little fellowship meeting in Aldergate Street that there came to him that overwhelming experience that warmed his heart, and sent him forth like a flame of fire to set the kingdom on a blaze. It was this glowing experience that led him to form the Methodist Society—significant word—divided into smaller companies called Classes, in each of which there were about twelve members. It was that sense of the vital necessity of fellowship both for ourselves and for others that made him pen this letter :

' There was one thing when I was with you that gave me pain ; you are not in the Society. But why not ? Is not this the way to enter into the spirit, and share the blessing, of a Christian community ?

' Perhaps you will say, '' I am joined in affection.'' True, but not to so good effect. This imperfect union

is not so encouraging to the people, not so strengthen-
ing to the preachers

'O delay no longer, for the sake of the work, for
the sake of the world, for the sake of your brethren.
There is something not easily explained in the fellowship of the Spirit which we enjoy with a society of
living Christians.

'But you say, "I do not care to meet a class; I find
no good in it." Suppose even you find even a dislike,
a loathing of it ; may not this be natural, or even
diabolical. In spite of this, break through, make a
fair trial. It is but a lion in the way. Meet only
six times (with previous prayer) and see if it do not
vanish away. But if it be a cross, still bear it for
the sake of your brethren.'

And the modern testimony is equally convincing.
Members of the Fellowship of the Kingdom movement gladly testify to the discoveries of God in
Christ Jesus that they have made as they have
thought, prayed, and talked together in their Groups.

The Rev. Harry Bisseker and Mr. Basil Mathews
in their book, *Fellowship in Thought and Prayer*, have
shown the rich discoveries of the leading and guidance
of a living God as they have met together with one
accord in one place.

The Oxford Group movement is bearing eloquent
witness to-day. Young Methodist undergraduates of
Cambridge have just issued a notable contribution
to the literature of the great theme, *A Group Speaks*,
in which they tell how they faced in fellowship this
searching question, 'Is the full, rich, evangelical
experience God's purpose for every man ?' They
found, to their dismay and shame that they did not

possess it, but they prayed together, devoured Paul and Wesley, and joined ' The Sect of Seekers.' The quest thus pursued in common brought thrilling unexpected and triumphant experiences. In various ways, for, as George Macdonald finely puts it, Jesus comes to us ' down His own secret stair,' they entered into the glowing New Testament experience of God in Christ Jesus. They found a golden bond of sympathy and understanding with each other, because they had become all one in Christ Jesus. They discovered the answer to Charles Wesley's prayer :

> Touched by the loadstone of Thy love,
>   Let all our hearts agree,
> And ever toward each other move,
>   And ever move toward Thee.

Fellowship first produced, and then amazingly enriched their transforming and growing experience.

Let him that readeth understand this reminder of the great little book, *Fellowship in Thought and Prayer* : ' Great movements in the world's history, associated as they are in the popular conception with the leadership of some powerful personality, can generally be traced in origin to the seed plot of some group of men whose fellowship in thought and often in prayer has itself been the nursery of that man's power of great leadership. John Woolman moving in his circle in America, and Wilberforce with his friends in England, debated and developed those germinal ideas which destroyed on the battlefields of America and in the Parliament of Britain the slavery that was arraigned first at the judgement bar of the Christian conscience. John Henry Newman

in concert with the flaming souls of Hurrell Froude
and the others of their group, nursed and fanned
the sparks that blazed out in the Oxford Movement.
Mazzini and his comrades proclaimed and fought for
the twin doctrines of nationality and liberty that
now begin to govern the world. The Gottesfreunde
similarly prepared the mind of Teutonic Europe for
the stormy message of Luther. The Holy Club
meeting in Wesley's room in Lincoln College toughened
the fibre and speeded and strengthened the indomit-
able wills that transformed England. Francis of
Assisi with his group of Poor Brothers gave Europe
such a vision of divine light on earth as she had not
seen before nor has witnessed since. And above all
stands that first Fellowship which moved through
the villages of Judea and by the cornfields and lake
side of Galilee and then went out to ' turn the world
upside down ! '

DAILY READINGS

1. Ephesians iv. 1-6.
2. Malachi iii. 16 ; Matthew xviii. 19, 20.
3. Philemon 2 ; Romans xvi. 5 ; 1 Cor. xvi. 15-19.
4. Mark iii. 14 ; Acts i. 12-14.
5. Acts ii. 1-4, 44-47.
6. Acts iv. 23-31.

QUESTIONARY

1. ' Fellowship is to the higher life what food is to the natural life—without it every power flags and at last perishes ' (Hort). Discuss and apply this.
2. Dr. Mott wrote that at the Jerusalem Conference there was ' generated an atmosphere in which it became possible to receive fresh mandates from the ever-creative God.' How can such an atmosphere be generated in your group ?
3. What are the fundamentals of fellowship ? Think this out together and then obey.

PRAYER AND THE NEW EXPERIENCE

VII

PRAYER AND THE NEW EXPERIENCE

THE first Christians possessed this supreme characteristic, that they were Christians who knew the value of believing prayer and gave themselves resolutely to its continual practice. The Church was filled with divine life and quenchless fire because it tirelessly pursued the pathway of hallowed communion with the living God and poured out its very soul in a fruitful and effective ministry of intercession. Prayer was to them the great essential if they required guidance, desired strength, needed grace. By prayer they strove to discover the divine mind and purpose ere they planned any new enterprise or embarked upon any fresh adventure.

They prayed when they met to fill the vacancy in their ranks caused by the tragic end of the traitor Judas Iscariot. They were gathered together with one accord and had continued steadfastly in prayer in the days that preceded the marvellous experience of the day of Pentecost. After that memorable crisis they continue steadfastly in the prayers. When Peter and John returned from the council to their own company they prayed, and the place wherein they were gathered together was shaken. They prayed before laying hands upon the seven deacons. Peter and John prayed that the Samaritan converts might receive the Holy Spirit. Saul of Tarsus prayed after the dazzling encounter on the Damascus road. Cornelius, the Gentile army officer, prayed to God alway, and, as he knelt, there came the clear and insistent message that he should send to Joppa for Peter, whose quiet prayer on the housetop was preparing him to take a step that was momentous in the history of the development of the Christian Church. It was prayer that brought Peter out of prison when escape seemed, humanly speaking, to be utterly impossible. Although the faith of the members of that little band was feeble, for they could not believe that their prayers had really and truly been answered, it was strong enough to cause them to sacrifice hours of sleep, and, after all, that is not a bad test of belief in the efficacy and power of intercession. They believed, and their Lord helped their unbelief. The Church at Antioch prayed before sending forth Barnabas and Paul on their first great missionary enterprise. At Miletus, Paul prayed with the elders of the Ephesian Church when he bade them farewell. On the island of Melita, Paul prayed over the father of Publius before he placed his healing hands upon the sufferer.

The members of the early Church with joy accepted literally the promise of Jesus, ' If ye shall ask anything in My name, I will do it. . . . Ask, and ye shall receive, that your joy may be full.' Paul sometimes had grave reason to mourn over the Churches that were so dear to his large heart, but he could always be confident that their prayer life was strong, and, being sure of that, he was very certain that they would grow in grace and that they would inevitably triumph over their ignorance, weakness, childishness, folly, and sin. He declared again and again that he set the highest value upon the Churches' intercessions for him, and was thereby immeasurably fortified as he pitted himself against apparently overwhelming adversaries, and addressed himself to his gigantic tasks of preaching, teaching, and debate. The Church has never had such a stalwart son as Paul, and it is deeply significant that we find him always stressing the vital need of prayer. The members of the early Church did not indulge in profound and protracted discussions concerning the value of prayer. They knew full well that mere academic debate leads only to a blind alley. They practised prayer, and were led triumphantly along the shining highways of the life of the Spirit. Paul and James might differ as to the precise value of faith—a difference that was merely superficial—but they were united in their belief in the value and necessity of prayer.

If we recall the triumphs won in widely differing spheres by Hudson Taylor, George Müller, Forbes Robinson and ' Praying ' Hyde of India, in recent days, we have a powerful and challenging reminder of the power of believing intercession. The members of the Cambridge Group were led through their revitalizing experience to discover the need of ' keen and disciplined prayer.'

Dr. J. R. Mott, who has done so much for the spiritual life of students all over the world, has borne this testimony : ' For many years it has been my practice in travelling among the nations to make a study of the sources of the spiritual movements which are doing most to vitalize and transform individuals and communities. At times it has been difficult to discover the hidden spring, but invariably where I have had the time and patience to do so, I have found it in an intercessory prayer-life of great reality.'

Too often prayer is lifeless, perfunctory and formal, because of the utter lack of reality. When the Cambridge Group visited young people in a church at ' Overbury ' they found that many of them, even though they were regular worshippers and workers, did not know how to pray. One confessed that nine times out of ten he might as well have been praying to the bed-post. But when the sense of the presence of Jesus comes as a new and rich experience prayer is immediately lifted to a loftier level. We are in heavenly places with Christ Jesus, a present help. We realize that prayer is much more than pleading, necessary and valuable though importunity be, as Jesus taught in the parables of the Friend at Midnight and the Unjust Judge. It is also a quiet sitting, like charmed and attentive Mary, listening to what our Lord has to disclose to us of His lovely secrets and His wondrous plans and purposes for our poor lives. When we have discovered that Jesus is an ever present Friend, we shall learn to be still and silent that we, with every faculty of the soul tuned and alert, may catch the faintest whisper of His gracious voice. The ancient promise is, ' I will guide thee with mine eye,' and we must needs be close and fully awake to catch that tender direction.

Dr. J. H. Jowett spoke out of the fulness of know-ledge, when he said, ' I think that the Church needs a more restful disposition in the ministry of prayer. I am amazed at the want of restfulness in our communion with the Lord. I do not speak of our unnecessary loudness, but of the feverish uncertainty, the strained and painful clutch and cleaving, the perspiring pleading which is half-suggestive of unbelief. Let me say it in great reverence, and not in a spirit of idle and careless criticism, when I listen to some prayers I find it difficult to realize that we are speaking to the One who said, " Behold, I stand at the door and knock ; if any man hear My voice, and open the door, I will come in to him, and sup with him, and he with Me." Our strained and restless prayers do not suggest the quiet opening of a door, they rather suggest a frenzied and fearful prisoner, hallooing to a God who has turned His back upon our door, and the sound of whose retreating footsteps is lessening in the far-away. We need a firmer and quieter assurance while we pray. Yes, even in our supplications it is needful to " rest in the Lord." Perhaps it would be a good thing for many of us in our praying seasons if we were to say less and to listen more. " I will hear what God the Lord will speak." Listening might bring restfulness where speech would only inflame us. It is not an insignificant thing that the marginal rendering of that lovely phrase " Rest in the Lord," is just this, " Be silent unto the Lord." '

For those who have entered into the joyous experience of the New Testament atmosphere, Jesus is so real that prayer is no frantic shouting across wide and misty gulfs in the hope that perchance someone is there who may give ear to our cries. It is rather a quiet, tender, intimate talk with a Friend who knows us through and through, who can interpret our silence, who is the Lover who sees in secret and openly gives us His reward, and, shining into our hearts, bids us 'go in peace.' That experience is not simply for the few, the choice and cloistered saints, it is for all men and women who toil and struggle in the rushing life of to-day.

Dr. F. W. Boreham has told an exquisite story of one who entered into the new experience and in so doing recreated his prayer life. A minister visiting one of his people, an old Scot who was very ill, noticed on the other side of the bed a chair placed as if it had just been vacated.

'Well, Donald,' said the minister, glancing at it, 'I see that I'm not your first visitor.'

The sick man looked up in surprise, so the minister pointed to the empty chair.

'Ah,' said the sufferer, 'I'll tell you about the chair. Years ago I found it impossible to pray. I often fell asleep on my knees, I was so tired. And if I kept awake I could not control my thoughts from wandering. One day I was so worried that I spoke to my minister about it. He told me not to worry about kneeling down. "Just sit down," he said, "and put a chair opposite to you, imagine Jesus is in it, and talk to Him as you would to a friend."

'And,' the Scotsman added, 'I have been doing that ever since. So now you know why the chair stands like that.'

A week later the daughter of the old Scot drove up to the minister's house. She was shown into the study, and when the minister came in she sobbed out her news, 'Father died in the night. I had no idea that death could be so near. I had just gone to lie down for an hour or two. He seemed to be sleeping so comfortably. And when I went back he was dead. He hadn't moved since I saw him before, except that *his hand was out on the empty chair by the side of the bed*. Do you understand?' 'Yes,' said the minister, 'I understand.'

That grand old saint had learned the secret of true prayer.

DAILY READINGS

1. Acts xii. 1-19.
2. James v. 13-18.
3. Colossians iv. 2-4, 12.
4. Romans xv. 30-33 ; Hebrews xiii. 18, 19.
5. 2 Cor. i. 3-11.
6. Acts i. 14 ; ii. 42 ; xiii. 1-3.

QUESTIONARY

1. Frank Fitful says, ' I only pray when I feel like it.' Can you help him ?
2. How can we make our prayer-life more real ?
3. If Paul were a member of your Church, how do you think he would proceed to strengthen its worth and witness ?

THE CROSS AND THE NEW EXPERIENCE

VIII

THE CROSS AND THE NEW EXPERIENCE

THE death of Jesus ought never to be separated from His life, for the story of the life and death is woven without seam. Calvary was the culmination of His life of sacrifice which began when, in the manger of Bethlehem, He

> Emptied Himself of all but love,

and which lasted through the silent years at Nazareth and the brief years of public ministry. He Himself led the way for His disciples and took up His cross daily.

Sadhu Sundar Singh, in one of his vivid parables, has thus expressed this truth : ' I once saw a sweeper carrying a pan of ordure in one hand, the stench of which almost made me vomit. But the sweeper was so used to it that with his spare hand he was holding food to his mouth and eating it. Just so, we are so habituated to the sin and evil of the world that we live in it quite unconcerned. But Christ would have felt in the midst of it as I felt when the sweeper passed me. Accordingly, it is a mistake to think of the suffering of Christ as being confined to the Crucifixion. Christ was thirty-three years upon the Cross.'

However widely we may differ in our interpretation of the meaning of the Cross—and surely, in the presence of that Cross theological wrangling ought to be impossible and the voice of recrimination be hushed to awed and devout silence—we cannot escape the fact that those in the early Church who had entered into the transforming experience put the Cross in the forefront of their preaching. In so doing she was taking no primrose path, but a hard and thorny way. It was the preaching of the contemptible Cross that alienated and disgusted many a hearer. Paul had to write : ' No man speaking in the spirit of God saith Jesus is anathema.' There were many who did declare that by His death upon the tree of shame Jesus had become anathema (accursed). Therefore when Paul wrote to the Galatians he explained this : ' Christ redeemed us from the curse of the law, having become a curse for us ; for it is written, Cursed is every one that hangeth on a tree.' He reminded the Corinthian Christians that when he came among them he determined to make Jesus the crucified the alpha and omega of his message even though it was a stumbling block to the Jews and arrant nonsense to the Greeks. He proved that he was right. The long course of history is on his side. It is significant that the early Churches gained their amazing triumphs, not by popular preaching, but by unpopular preaching!

It is not clear whether the familiar words of John iii. 16, proceeded from the mouth of Jesus or from the pen of the evangelist. But here, at all events, we need not spend time in debate concerning the source. Jesus always taught the glad lesson of the true and rich Fatherhood of God. If John added these words in an outburst of thankfulness, a doxology that could not be restrained but which had to find its expression even upon his sacred page, then the addition plainly illustrates how in the transforming experience the members of the early Church had begun to pierce through the veiling shadows to the loving heart of God the Father. He was like Jesus, and that revelation was enough. The ancient sacrifices spoke of an angry God who needed to be propitiated by the blood of victims ' on Jewish altars slain.' The Cross of Christ revealed a God of love, whose love, so tender and so vast and so deep, could go even to the Cross of Calvary.

The early Church knew ' the fellowship of His sufferings.' The Cross was their way of life. Persistent persecution was their common lot. They were aliens from the commonwealth of Israel, though they loved their countrymen with a deathless love, and the fires of patriotic devotion ever flamed and blazed in their breasts. Families were sundered, and many a tear must have been shed over the shattering of prized and precious friendships. They suffered loss of business, workmen were dismissed to face poverty and hunger. Some paid an even costlier price for their new experience, for theirs was prison, exile, and death. But their loyalty remained unshaken. They had caught the spirit of their redeeming Lord, and, like Him, they ' endured the cross, despising shame.'

Throughout the ages the Cross has been the ' piercing point of the gospel.' Its proclamation has brought conviction of sin followed by full and free salvation. Bunyan wrote from the pages of his own transforming experience when he tells how Christian, having found that there was no other way of release from his burden found that it rolled away when he came to the Cross.

Robert Wilkinson, one of Wesley's preachers, describes his deep conviction of sin and his midnight wanderings in the fields bewailing his desperate state. But he writes on Sunday, July 12, 1767 : ' Joseph Watson preached in the chapel in Weardale. He gave out that hymn,

> All ye that pass by,
> To Jesus draw nigh :
> To you is it nothing that Jesus should die ?
> Your ransom and peace,
> Your surety He is ;
> Come, see if there ever was sorrow like His.
>
> For you and for me
> He prayed on the tree :
> The prayer is accepted, the sinner is free.

' Then all within me cried out,

> That sinner am I,
> Who on Jesus rely,
> And come for the pardon God cannot deny.

' I then believed that God for Christ's sake had forgiven all my sins, and found that peace which arises from a sense of reconciliation. The people of God who knew my distress perceived by my countenance that the Lord was gracious to me, before I had the opportunity to tell them. I then went rejoicing home, and could not help telling what God had done for my soul.'

Or take a recent witness from Madras, recounted in the Report of the Wesleyan Methodist Missionary Society :

There was in Madaveram, a big village near Madras, a very dirty girl, absolutely hardened in dirt and sin. Try as she would, the Bible-woman could make no impression on her, could not induce her to clean either her body or her soul. During one of her visits, the Bible-woman showed some pictures to the women, amongst them being one of Jesus on the cross. The poor sin-stained girl was standing near looking on, and the Bible-woman, touched by a sense of her need, gave the picture into her hands and allowed her to keep it. The girl shortly after left Madaveram, and was away for some months.

One day when the Bible-woman was walking along the road, she met a very clean, happy-looking girl, who said, ' Salaam Ammal ; don't you know me ? '

The Bible-woman looked at her for some time, and then said : ' Well, you do remind me of a little girl who once lived here, but she was a dirty, bad girl.'

' Oh yes, I am she,' was the answer. ' When I left Madaveram I took the picture of Jesus with me. I often looked at it, and at last I couldn't bear to feel that He suffered such agonies for me—the wounds on His hands, side, and feet, and the dreadful behaviour of the people, and His dying on the cross, *and all for me so dirty and bad*. Now I love Him. He has changed me.'

Japan has its story of Tokichi Ishii, murderer and debauchee, who read in prison the story of the crucifixion for the first time, and whose heart was thereby pierced as if ' by a five-inch nail.' He went to death with a shining face and purified soul, saved by the Cross.

Sister Gladys Stephenson, of the new Union

Hospital in Hankow, tells of one of her patients, a printer by trade, who had prospered in his business but had squandered his money in evil living. He ' was greatly convicted of sin by the message of the Cross. When he realized that it was for his sins that Christ died, he broke down and wept, and confessed to the evangelist all his past wrong-doing. He was assured that forgiveness awaited true repentance and day by day he learned to realize more what a new life in Christ Jesus might mean.'

From Northern Rhodesia the Rev. G. H. B. Sketchley sends this witness :

'An old woman was brought to me for baptism. She had been on trial for some years but was unable to learn very much, and she greatly desired to be baptized. I satisfied myself that she had the root of the matter in her, and then asked her why she so much desired to be baptized. Her reply was something like this : " I want to be allowed to take Communion. Jesus died for me, and I love Him, and this is what He commanded." I baptized her, and when she came up to take her first Communion, at the words, "The Blood of the Lord Jesus Christ which was shed for you," she bowed her head to the very ground, while the tears streamed down her face.'

And still the Cross exerts a mighty saving power in life and conduct. The new experience brings a fuller sense of sin, but it brings also a newer sense of the love of the Saviour and the magnificence of our salvation.

> Neither passion nor pride
> Thy Cross can abide,
> But melt in the fountain that streams from Thy side.

The transforming experience means for all who

have known it that the Cross is the only way of life.
That to find life, we must first lose it That the world
will not be won by men and women who follow afar
off, dilettanti in religion, but only by those who are
willing patiently, steadily, and teachably to follow
the call of Jesus and to pay the price.

> Shall Jesus bear the Cross alone
> And all the world go free ?

The Jerusalem Conference of 1928, really a Fellowship Group of Christian leaders from some fifty
countries, came to this searching and challenging
conclusion :

' We are persuaded that we and all Christian people
must seek a more heroic practice of the gospel. It
cannot be that our present complacency and our
moderation are a faithful expression of the mind of
Christ, and of the meaning of His Cross and Resurrection in the midst of the wrong and want and sin of our
modern world. As we contemplate the work with
which Christ has charged His Church, we who are
met here on the Mount of Olives, in sight of Calvary,
would take up for ourselves and summon those from
whom we come, and to whom we return, to take up
with us the Cross of Christ, and all that for which it
stands, and to go forth into the world to live in the
fellowship of His sufferings and by the power of His
Resurrection, in hope and expectation of His glorious
Kingdom '

DAILY READINGS

1. Revelation vii. 9-17.
2. John iii. 16 ; Romans v. 1-11.
3. 1 John iv. 7-14.
4. 1 Corinthians i. 17-25.
5. 1 Peter i. 13-21.
6. Mark xv. 21-41.

QUESTIONARY

1. ' When I survey the wondrous Cross.'
   Write down and ponder upon some of its wonders.
2. Discuss the place of Holy Communion in the Christian life.
3. ' If any man will come after Me, let him . . .'
   Complete that sentence, and face its searching call.